PEGASUS ENCYCLOPEDIA LIBRARY

Environment

ATMOSPHERE, WEATHER AND CLIMATE

Edited by: Pallabi B. Tomar, Hitesh Iplani
Managing editor: Tapasi De
Designed by: Vijesh Chahal, Anil Kumar, Rohit Kumar
Illustrated by: Suman S. Roy, Tanoy Choudhury
Colouring done by: Vinay Kumar, Kiran Kumari & Pradeep Kumar

CONTENTS

What is atmosphere?

The Earth is surrounded by a blanket of air called the **atmosphere**. The atmosphere is made up of various gases that act as a protective shield for the Earth and allow life to exist. Without it, we would be burned by the intense heat of the sun during the day or frozen by the very low temperatures at night.

It is made of air which is a mixture of oxygen (21 per cent), nitrogen (78 per cent), carbon dioxide (0.037 per cent) and other gases such as hydrogen, helium, argon, neon, krypton, xenon and ozone. It also contains water vapour. These gases are densest at the Earth's surface and get less dense with increasing height. The atmosphere in the lowest 15 km above the surface of the Earth is the thickest and as one goes higher the layer of atmosphere becomes thinner.

Ecosystems (an interrelated community of plants, animals and bacteria) on the Earth are protected by the atmosphere, which absorbs ultraviolet solar radiation and reduces extreme conditions of temperature between day and night.

Astonishing fact

The mixture of gases in the atmosphere has taken over 4.5 billion years to evolve!

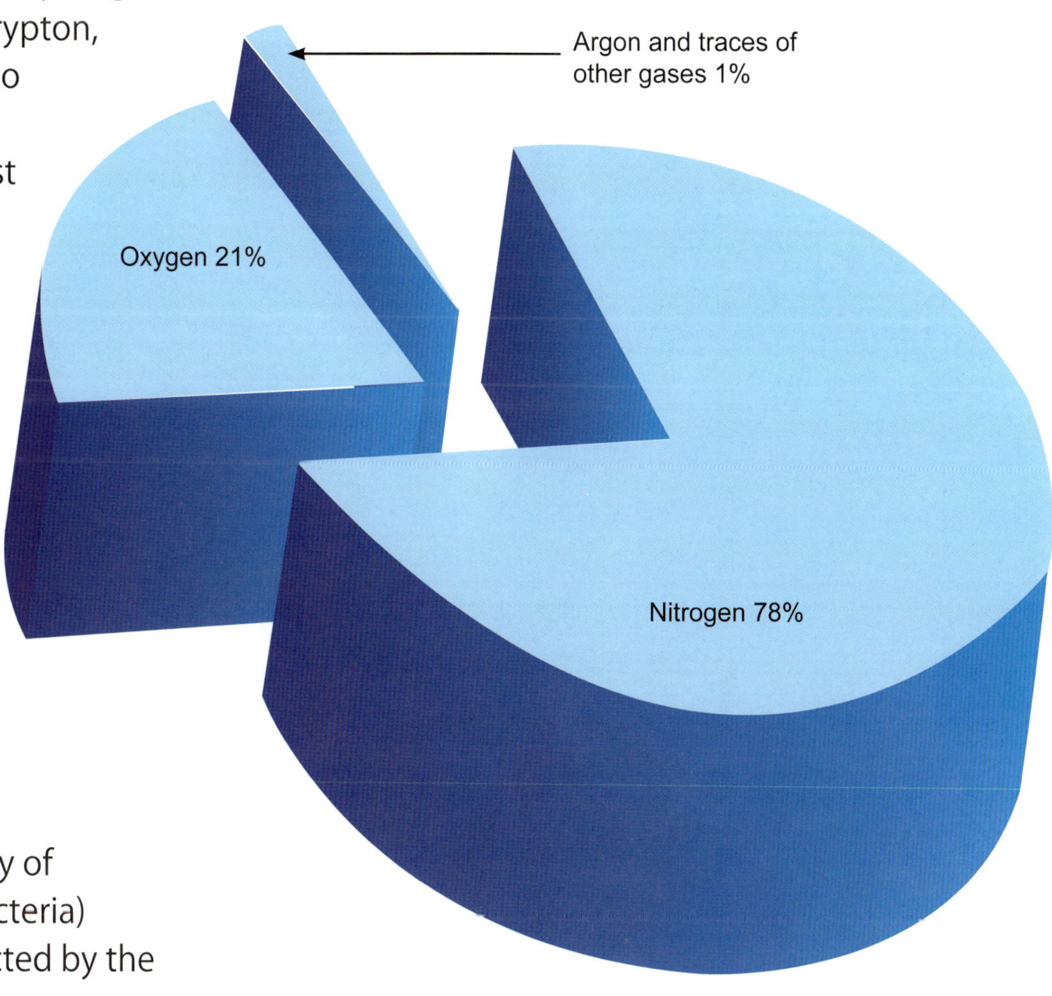

More than three quarters of the atmosphere is made up of nitrogen and most of the rest is oxygen. However, it is the remaining 1 per cent, which is a mixture of carbon dioxide, water vapour and ozone that not only produces important weather features such as cloud and rain, but also has considerable influence on the overall climate of the Earth, through mechanisms such as the greenhouse effect and global warming.

Oxygen is essential to life because it allows us to breathe. Some of the oxygen has changed over time to ozone. The ozone layer filters out the sun's harmful rays. Recently, there have been many studies on how humans have caused a hole in the ozone layer.

Humans are also affecting Earth's atmosphere through the greenhouse effect. Due to increases in gases, like carbon dioxide, that trap heat being radiated from the Earth, scientists believe that the atmosphere is having trouble staying in balance creating the greenhouse effect.

Astonishing fact

Gravity holds the atmosphere close to the Earth. It is divided into various layers according to differences in temperature.

Layers of the atmosphere

The atmosphere consists of five layers held around the planet by the force of gravity. As you move upwards through the layers, atmospheric pressure decreases rapidly with height and the air temperature also changes. It is these, more complicated, changes in temperature which are used to divide the atmosphere into the layers described below.

Astonishing fact

Nearly all of the water vapour and dust particles in the atmosphere are in the troposphere. That is why most clouds are found in this lowest layer too.

Troposphere

The troposphere is the lowest layer of Earth's atmosphere. The troposphere starts at Earth's surface and goes up to a height of 7 to 20 km above sea level. Most of the mass (about 75-80 per cent) of the atmosphere is in the troposphere. Almost all weather conditions occur within this layer. Air is warmest at the bottom of the troposphere near ground level. Higher up it gets colder. Air pressure and the density of the air are also less at high altitudes.

The boundary between the top of the troposphere and the stratosphere (the layer above it) is called the **tropopause**. The height of the tropopause depends on latitude, season and whether it is day or night. Near the equator, the tropopause is about 20 km above sea level. In winter near the poles the tropopause is much lower. It is about 7 km high.

Stratosphere

The stratosphere is the second layer of air above the Earth's surface and extends to a height of 50 km. It is here that we find the ozone layer. The ozone layer absorbs much of the sun's harmful radiation that would otherwise be dangerous to plants and animal life.

This layer lies directly above the troposphere and is about 35 km deep. It extends from about 15 to 50 km above the Earth's surface. The lower portion of the stratosphere has a nearly constant temperature but in the upper portion, the temperature increases with altitude because of the absorption of sunlight by ozone. This temperature increase with altitude is the opposite of the situation in the troposphere.

Air is roughly a thousand times thinner at the top of the stratosphere than it is at the sea level. Due to this, jet aircraft and weather balloons reach their maximum operational altitudes within the stratosphere.

The transition boundary which separates the stratosphere from the mesosphere is called the **stratopause** and the transition boundary that separates mesosphere and thermosphere is called **mesopause**. The regions of the stratosphere and the mesosphere, along with the stratopause and mesopause, are called the **middle atmosphere** by scientists.

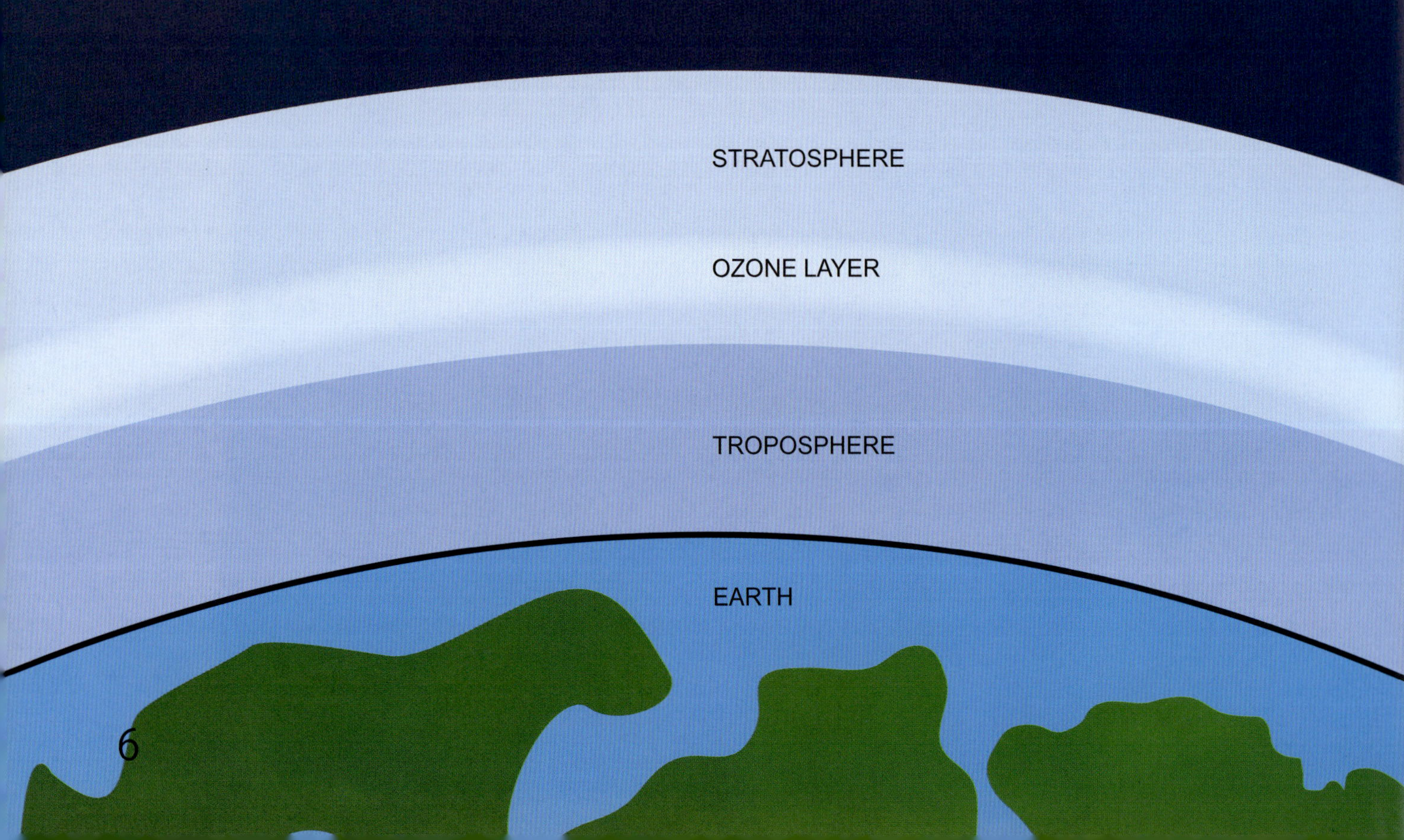

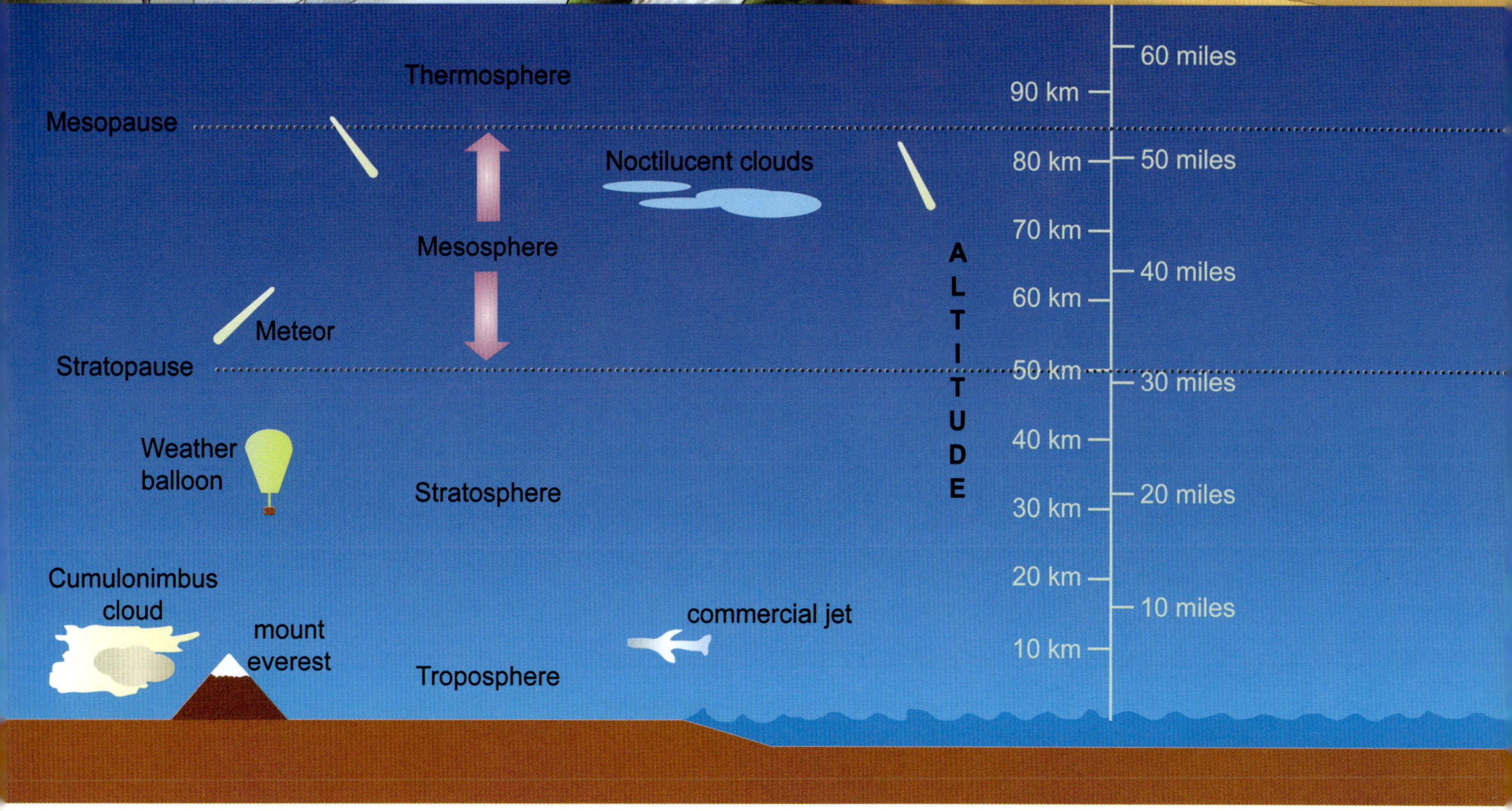

Thermosphere
Mesopause
Noctilucent clouds
Mesosphere
Meteor
Stratopause
Weather balloon
Stratosphere
Cumulonimbus cloud
mount everest
commercial jet
Troposphere
ALTITUDE
90 km, 80 km, 70 km, 60 km, 50 km, 40 km, 30 km, 20 km, 10 km
60 miles, 50 miles, 40 miles, 30 miles, 20 miles, 10 miles

Mesosphere

The mesosphere is the third highest layer in our atmosphere, occupying the region 50 km to 80 km above the surface of the Earth, above the troposphere and stratosphere. It is below the thermosphere. The mesosphere is separated from the stratosphere by the stratopause and from the thermosphere by the mesopause.

Temperatures in the mesosphere drop with increasing altitude to about -100°C. The mesosphere is the coldest of the atmospheric layers. In fact, it is colder than Antarctica's lowest recorded temperature. It is cold enough to freeze water vapour into ice clouds. You can see these clouds if sunlight hits them after sunset. They are called **Noctilucent Clouds** (NLC). NLCs are most readily visible when the sun is from 4 to 16 degrees below the horizon.

The mesosphere is also the layer in which a lot of meteors burn up while entering the Earth's atmosphere. From the Earth they are seen as shooting stars.

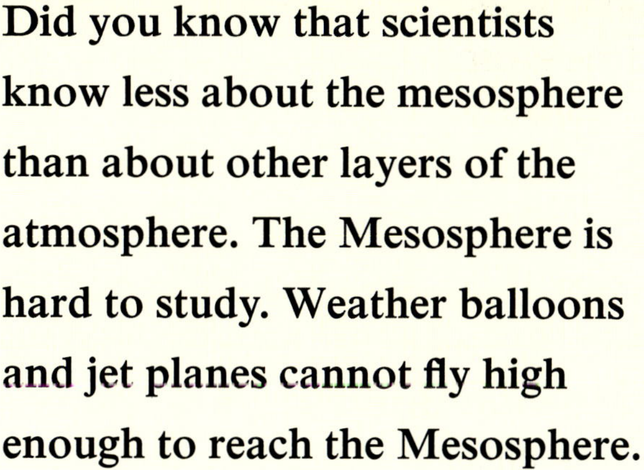

Astonishing fact

Did you know that scientists know less about the mesosphere than about other layers of the atmosphere. The Mesosphere is hard to study. Weather balloons and jet planes cannot fly high enough to reach the Mesosphere.

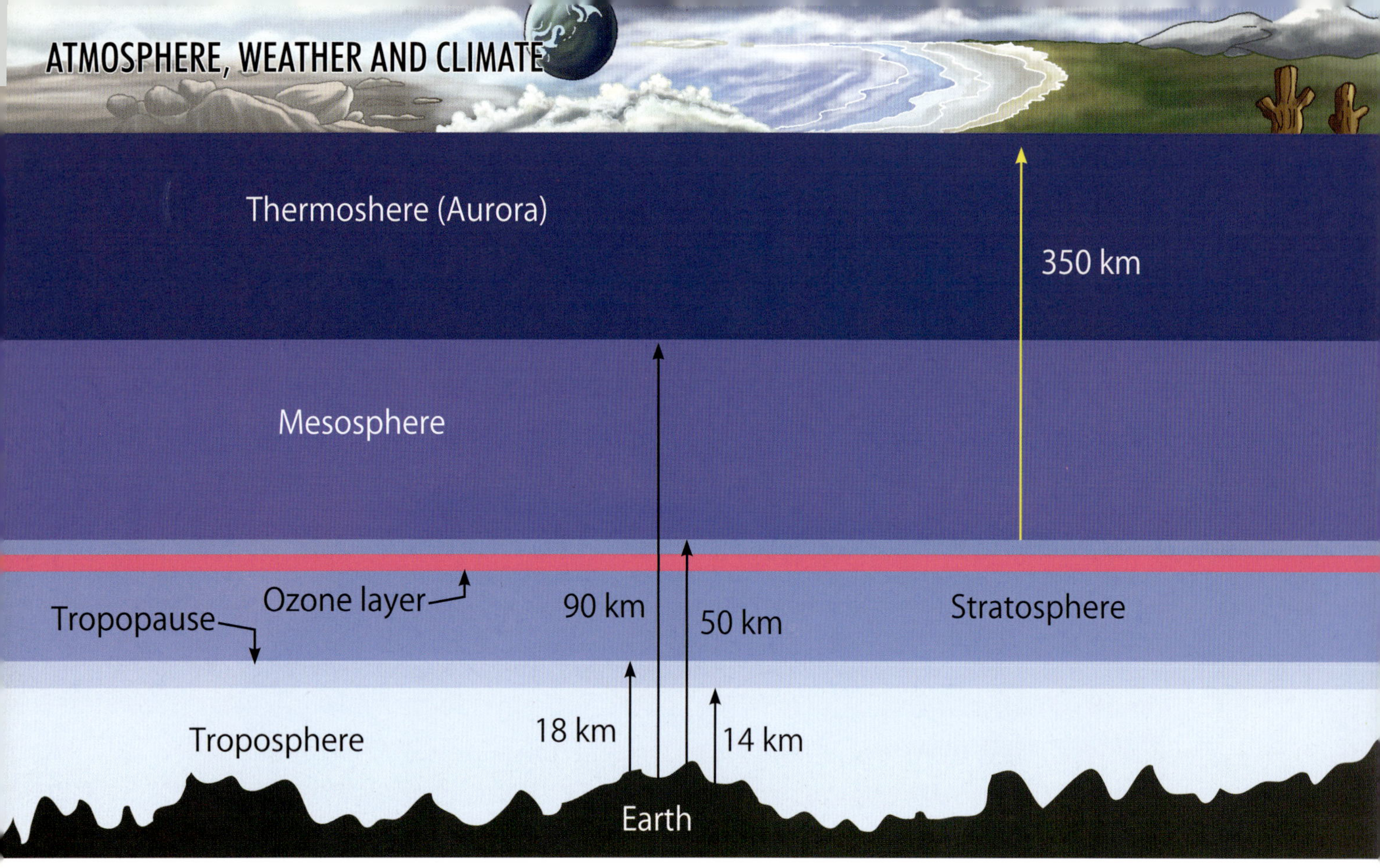

Thermosphere

The thermosphere is the fourth layer of the atmosphere. It extends from about 90 km to between 500 and 1,000 km above our planet. Space shuttles fly in this area and it is also where the aurora lights are found. Auroras are wispy curtains of light caused when the sun strikes gases in the atmosphere above the poles. The boundary between the thermosphere and the exosphere above is called the **thermopause**.

Temperatures climb sharply in the lower thermosphere (below 200 to 300 km altitude), then levels off and maintains a fairly steady temperature with increasing altitude above that height. Solar activity strongly influences temperature in the thermosphere. The thermosphere is typically about 200° C hotter in the daytime than at night, and roughly 500° C hotter when the sun is very active than at other times. Temperatures in the upper thermosphere can range from about 500° C to 2,000° C or higher!

The lower part of the thermosphere, from 80 to 550 km above the Earth's surface, contains the ionosphere. Beyond the ionosphere extending out to perhaps 10,000 km is the exosphere or outer thermosphere, which gradually merges into space.

Much of the X-ray and UV radiation from the sun is absorbed by the Thermosphere.

Exosphere

The exosphere is the outermost layer of the atmosphere. It extends from the thermopause to 10,000 km above the Earth. This is the upper limit of our atmosphere. The atmosphere here merges into space in the extremely thin air. Air atoms and molecules are constantly escaping to space from the exosphere. In this region of the atmosphere, hydrogen and helium are the prime components and are only present at extremely low densities. This is the area where many satellites orbit the Earth.

Astonishing fact

Atmosphere's balance is disturbed by human activity which causes greenhouse effect, global warming, air contamination, ozone belt destruction and acid rains.

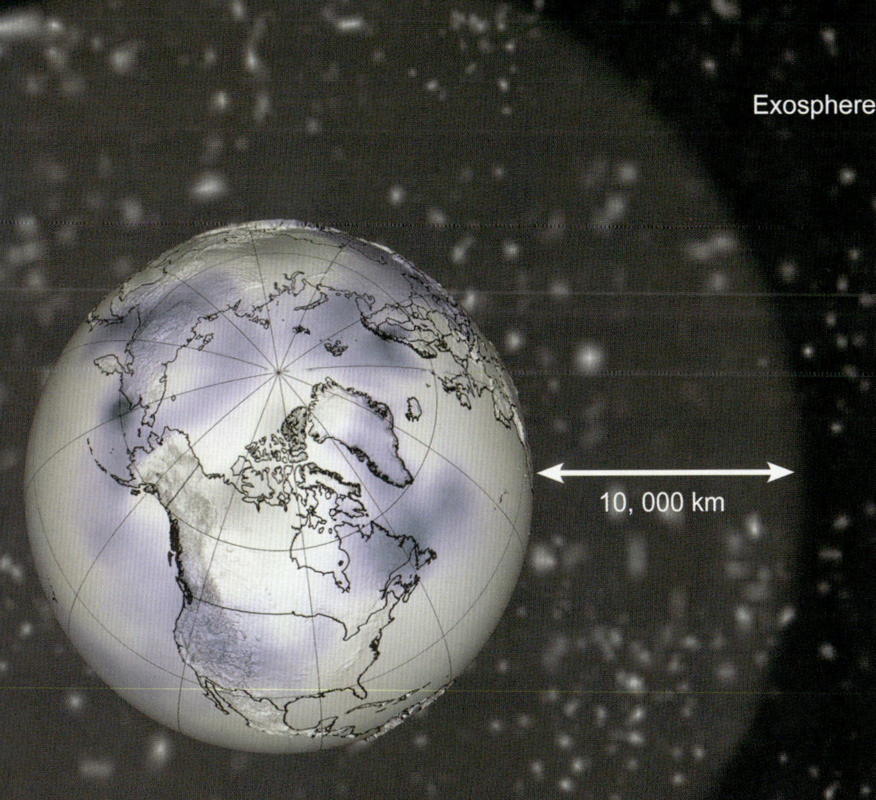

Other layers

Ionosphere

Scientists call the ionosphere an extension of the thermosphere. So technically, the ionosphere is not another atmospheric layer. The ionosphere represents less than 0.1 per cent of the total mass of the Earth's atmosphere. Even though it is such a small part, it is extremely important.

The upper atmosphere is ionized by solar radiation. That means the sun's energy is so strong at this level, that it breaks apart molecules. So there ends up being electrons floating around and molecules which have lost or gained electrons. When the sun is active, more and more ionization happens!

Different regions of the ionosphere make long distance radio communication possible by reflecting the radio waves back to Earth. It is also home to auroras. Temperatures in the ionosphere just keep getting hotter as you go up.

Astonishing fact

The large number of free electrons in the ionosphere allows the propagation of electromagnetic waves. Radio signals, form of electromagnetic radiation can be 'bounced' off the ionosphere allowing radio communication over long distances.

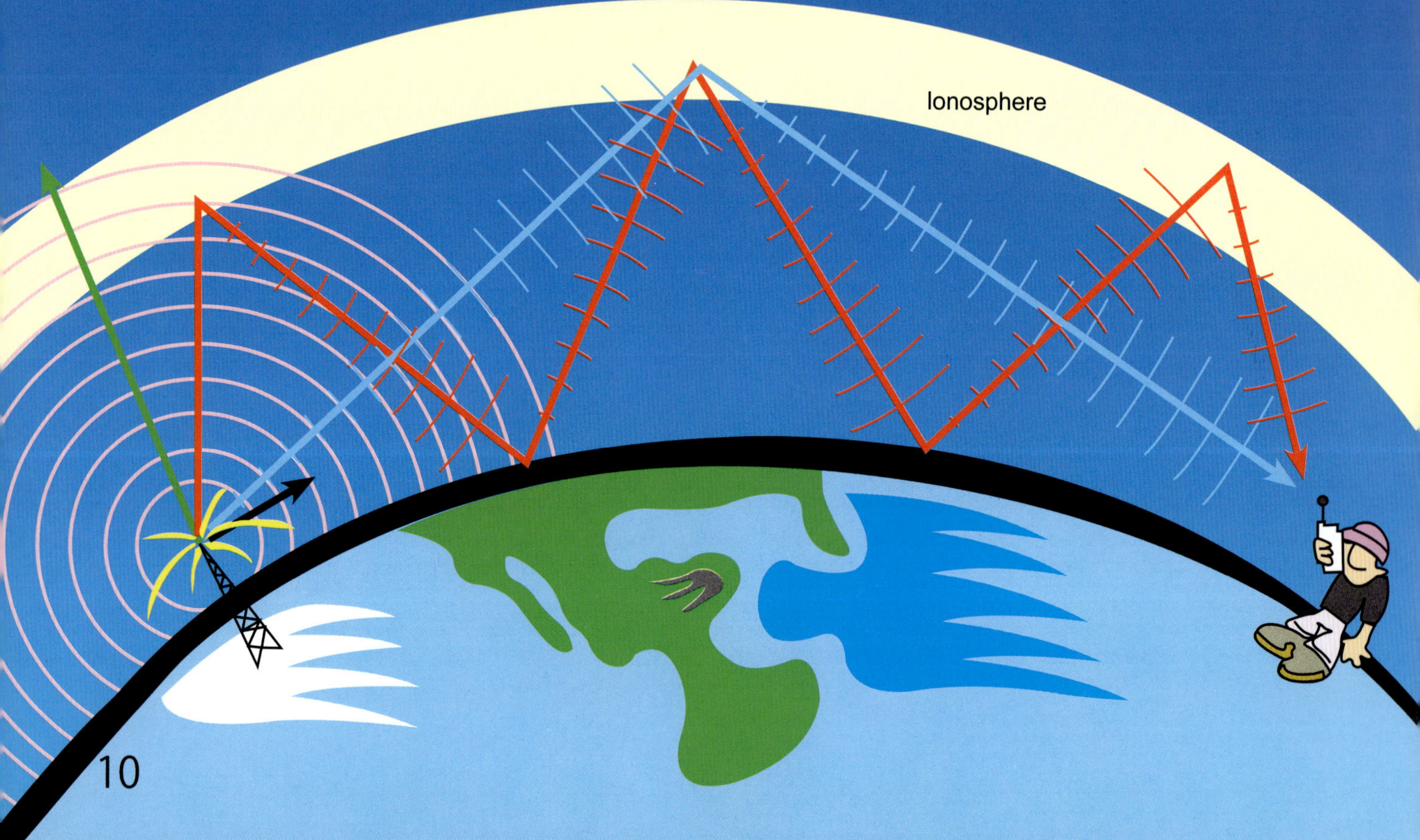

Ozone layer

The ozone layer is a layer of ozone particles scattered between 19 and 30 km up in the Earth's atmosphere in a region called the stratosphere. Without the ozone layer, ultraviolet (UV) radiation from the sun would not be stopped from entering the Earth's atmosphere and causing damage to most living species.

Ozone and oxygen molecules in the stratosphere absorb ultraviolet light from the sun, providing a shield that prevents this radiation from passing to the Earth's surface. While both oxygen and ozone together absorb 95 to 99.9 per cent of the sun's ultraviolet radiation, only ozone effectively absorbs the most energetic ultraviolet light, known as UV-C and UV-B. This ultraviolet light can cause biological damage like skin cancer, tissue damage to eyes and plant tissue damage. The protective role of the ozone layer in the upper atmosphere is so vital that scientists believe life on land probably would not have evolved— and could not exist today— without it.

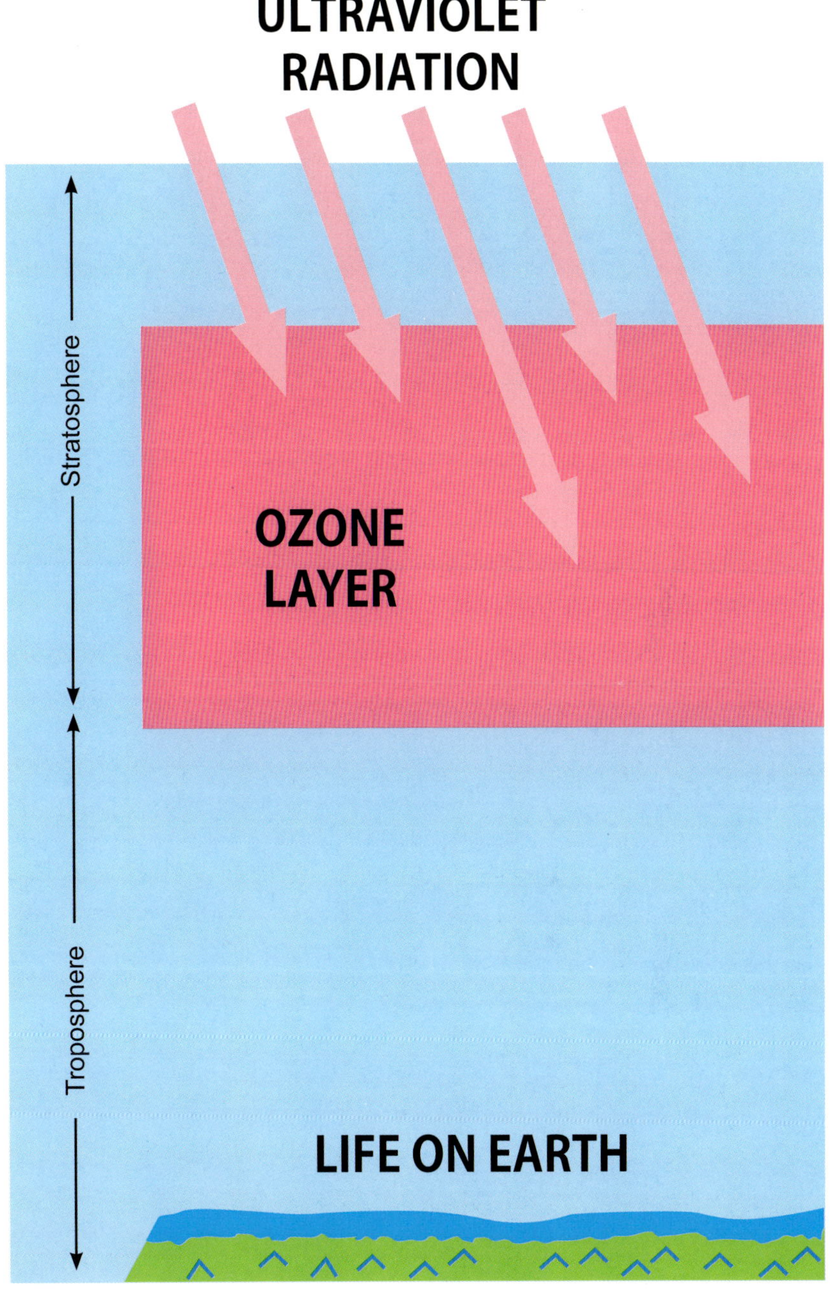

The frequency of skin cancers is increased by the thinning of the ozone layer. In 1985, a hole into the ozone layer was observed in Antarctica. In 1995, a similar hole was spotted into the ozone layer over the Arctic.

What is weather?

The term **weather** describes the state of the air, clouds and sunshine at a particular place and time; whether it is warm or cold, wet or dry, and how cloudy or windy it is. Most weather changes take place in the troposphere, the lowest layer of the atmosphere.

There are really a lot of components to weather. Weather includes sunshine, rain, cloud cover, winds, hail, snow, sleet, freezing rain, flooding, blizzards, ice storms, thunderstorms, steady rains from a cold front or warm front, excessive heat, heat waves and many more.

Astonishing fact

Al'Aziziyah in Libya has the highest recorded temperature on Earth at a sweltering 58 degree Celsius on the 13th Sept, 1922.

Weather changes each day because the air in our atmosphere is always moving, distributing energy from the sun. In most places in the world, the types of weather events also vary throughout the year as seasons change.

Types of weather

Weather, which is a temporary status of the atmosphere, varies with time and place and various types of weather can be seen in various parts of the world. Weather is never constant anywhere. It depends on the climatic conditions and changes occurring in the seasons too. Weather may be of different types, such as **coastal weather** in the oceanic regions, **hot weather** in the equatorial climate zones, **cold weather** in the polar climate zones and **mountain weather** in the hilly and mountainous regions of the world.

Astonishing fact

The lowest ever recorded world temperature was at Vostok Station, Antarctica on July 21, 1983. The temperature dropped to a bitter -89.6 degree Celsius!

Coastal weather

Coastal weather can be observed in the coastal or oceanic regions. The western coasts of the continents and the southeastern regions of Australia are characterized with the coastal climate. The southeastern Australia is located between the South Pacific Ocean and the Indian Ocean. One of the most prominent characteristics of coastal weather is that the temperature does not vary so much with the change of seasons throughout the year in these coastal areas. The climate of marine regions is never extreme.

Astonishing fact

The South Pole is the least sunny place getting only 182 days of sunshine.

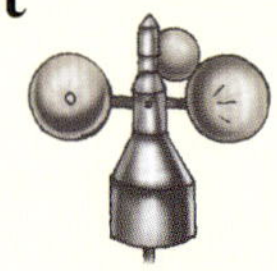

Hot weather

Extreme hot weather can be seen in the equatorial regions of the Earth. Throughout the year, the temperature remains very warm in these equatorial locations. The climate in equatorial regions is also characterized with a very damp and humid weather. The amount of rainfall is also very high throughout the year. Sometimes the temperature falls a little (only about 3 degree Celsius) in the winter months.

Astonishing fact

Yuma in the state of Arizona has over 4,000 hours of sunshine per year making it the sunniest place on the planet!

Astonishing fact

The highest snow fall ever recorded in a one year period was 31.1 m in Mount Rainier, Washington State, United States, between February 19, 1971 and February 18, 1972.

Cold weather

Cold weather can be observed in the polar climate zones. These regions are known for their extreme cold climates. The temperature remains almost same throughout the year in these Polar Regions.

Mountain weather

The weather in the mountainous regions is known as the mountain weather. The climate of those regions is generally cold enough. New Zealand comes under those high countries that enjoy the mountain weather conditions.

Weather instruments

Anemometer

The weather instrument called an **anemometer**, measures the wind speed. The anemometer has cups that spin in the wind to measure the wind speed. The faster the wind blows, the faster the cups spin. Every time a certain coloured cup passes by, it is counted as one revolution.

The first person who invented the anemometer was Leon Battista. He invented the anemometer in 1456. He recorded the amount of wind pushing against a flat plate that was joined to a spring. The first person, who invented the anemometer that used numbers to record the wind speed, was Robert Hook. He invented it in 1667.

Astonishing fact

The Earth experiences millions of lightning storms every year. They are incredible discharges of electricity from the atmosphere that can reach temperatures close to 30,000 °C.

Barometer

A **barometer** measures air pressure. It tells you whether the pressure is rising or falling. A rising barometer means sunny and dry conditions, while a falling barometer means stormy and wet conditions.

Evangelista Torricelli invented the first barometer in 1643. His barometer was a glass tube about 92 cm long. It was open on one end and closed on the other. He filled the tube with mercury and put the open end in a dish of mercury. When the air pressure was high, there was less space at the top of the tube. When the air pressure was low then there was more space in the top of the tube.

Astonishing fact

Everyday there are approximately 1,800 thunderstorms occurring in the Earth's atmosphere.

Hygrometer

The weather instrument called a hygrometer, measures the amount of moisture (water vapour) in the air. The hygrometer shows the moisture in the air which causes humidity.

Cardinal Nicholas de Cusa was the first inventor of the hygrometer. His hygrometer didn't really look like a weather instrument. The inventor just weighed some wool on a scale. When there was moisture in the air, it made the wool heavier because the wool sucked up the moisture from the air. But when it was dry, there was less moisture in the air, so the wool was lighter.

Astonishing fact

Raindrops are much smaller than we think. They range from 1/100 inch to 1/4 inch in diameter!

Rain gauge

The weather instrument called a **rain gauge**, measures the amount of rainfall. The way the rain gauge works is that water droplets fall into the rain gauge and then the amount of rainfall is measured with a type of measuring instrument such as a ruler. You have to make sure that you look straight at eye level, when you look at the water line inside of the container. The rain gauge works better when it's not hidden under trees or houses, because you don't want anything getting in the way of the falling rain.

The Chinese government recorded the rainfall during Chou's ruling of China over 3000 years ago! Also, around 400 B.C. rainfall was measured and recorded in India. These rainfall measurements were used for farming. Rain gauges were also used in Korea around 1442 A.D.

Raindrops fall between 3 and 8 m per second in still air. The range in speed depends on the size of the raindrop. Air friction breaks up raindrops when they exceed 28 km per hour.

Thermometer

The weather instrument called the **thermometer**, measures the air temperature. The mercury rises in the thermometer because it is heated. The mercury molecules move farther apart and faster when they are heated. The liquid falls in the tube when the mercury molecules are cold, because they move slower and closer together. The liquid is usually mercury, but alcohol is also used in some thermometers.

Astonishing fact

You can use pine cones to forecast the weather. The scales will close when rain is on the way!

The first person who invented the thermometer was Galileo Galilei. It was first invented in 1593. It was an upside-down tube in a dish of liquid. His open thermometer was affected by air pressure. Forty-eight years later a sealed-in thermometer was made.

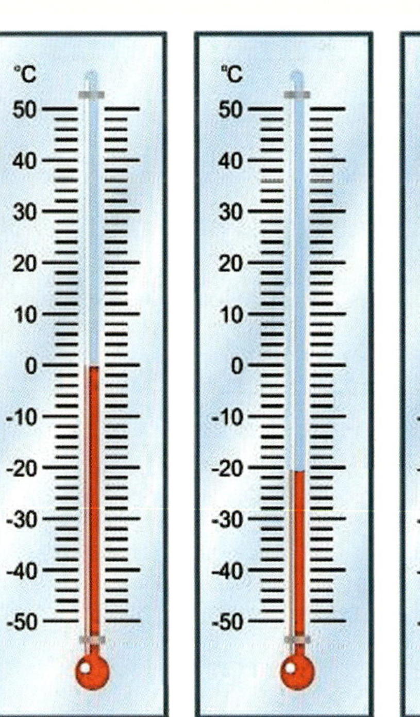

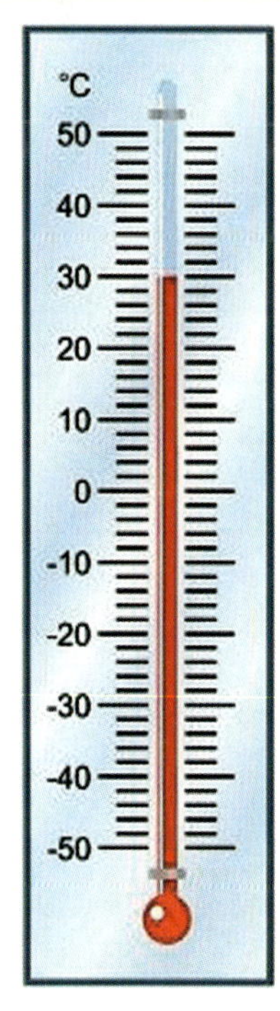

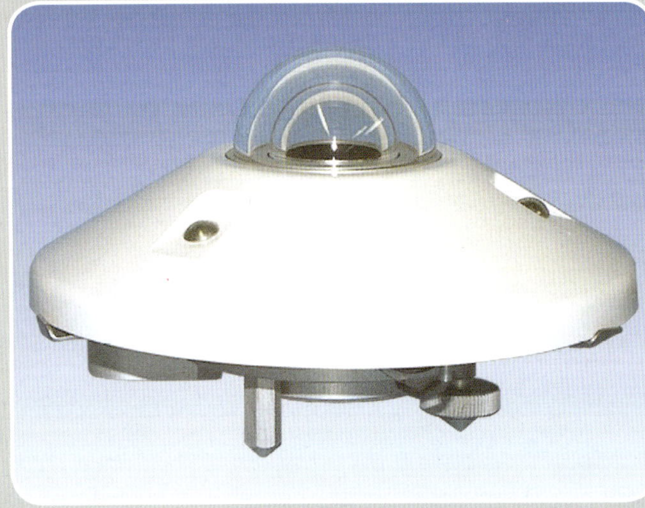

Pyranometer

The biggest clouds are cumulonimbus, climbing up to 9.7 km high and holding up to half a million tons of water.

Wind vane

The weather instrument called a **weather vane** or **wind vane**, works by pointing in the direction that the wind is blowing in. If the head of the arrow is pointing to the north-east, then the wind is coming from the north-east.

The wind vane was invented 3500 to 4000 years ago according to the ancient writings. The earliest weather vane was built by the astronomer named Adronicus. It had the figure of the Greek God Triton whose body was made up of the head and torso of a man and the tail of a fish. This weather vane was between 4 to 8 ft long.

Pyranometer

Solar radiation can affect weather. Although not commonly found in weather stations, **pyranometers** measure solar radiation.

Wind vane

What is climate?

Climate is the average weather usually taken over a 30 year time period for a particular region and time period. Climate is not the same as weather, but rather, it is the average pattern of weather for a particular region. Weather describes the short-term state of the atmosphere.

Climate describes the total of all weather occurring over a period of years in a given place. This includes average weather conditions, regular weather sequences (like winter, spring, summer, and fall), and special weather events (like tornadoes and floods). Climate tells us what it's usually like in the place where you live.

Climates vary from place to place and the countries around the world do not fit into specific categories of climate and weather. Many things influence a place's climate such as distance from the equator and the local topography (natural features). Mountain ranges can increase or decrease rainfall. Coastal areas often have a different climate than those of the inland. Climates also vary over time and change very gradually over decades and centuries.

Over the last 50 years, human activities, particularly the burning of fossil fuels (substances like coal and petroleum) have released sufficient quantities of carbon dioxide and other greenhouse gases to affect the global climate.

The climate where you live is called **regional climate**. To describe the regional climate of a place, people often tell what the temperatures are like over the seasons, how windy it is and how much rain or snow falls. The climate of a region depends on many factors including the amount of sunlight it receives, its height above sea level, the shape of the land, and how close it is to oceans. Since the equator receives more sunlight than the poles, climate varies depending on distance from the equator.

Global climate is a description of the climate of a planet as a whole, with all the regional differences averaged. Overall, global climate depends on the amount of energy received by the sun and the amount of energy that is trapped in the system. These amounts are different for different planets. Scientists who study Earth's climate and climatic changes, study the factors that affect the climate of our whole planet.

While the weather can change in just a few hours, climate changes over longer timeframes. Climate events, like El Nino, happen over several years, small-scale fluctuations happen over decades and larger climate changes happen over hundreds and thousands of years.

Köppen climate classification system

The Köppen climate classification system is the most widely used for classifying the world's climates. It was first published by German climatologist Wladimir Köppen in 1884, with several later modifications by Köppen himself notably in 1918 and 1936. Later, German climatologist Rudolf Geiger collaborated with Köppen and added changes to the classification system, which is thus sometimes referred to as the **Köppen–Geiger climate classification system.**

The Köppen system recognizes five major climate types based on the annual and monthly averages of temperature and precipitation. Each type is designated by a capital letter.

Tropical Moist Climate are known for their high temperatures year round and for their large amount of rain round the year.

Dry Climate are characterized by little rain and a huge daily temperature range. The two subgroups of this climate type are—**semiarid or steppe** and **arid or desert**.

In **Humid Middle Latitude Climates** have warm, dry summers and cool, wet winters.

Continental Climate can be found in the interior regions of large land masses. Total precipitation is not very high and seasonal temperatures vary widely.

Cold Climate are part of areas where ice is permanently present. Only about four months of the year have above freezing temperatures.

Climatology is the scientific study of climates which is defined as the average weather conditions over a period of time.

Tropical Moist Climate

Tropical moist climates extend northward and southward from the equator to about 15 to 25 degree of latitude. In these climates all months have average temperatures greater than 18 degree Celsius. Annual rainfall is greater than 1500 mm. Monthly temperature variations in this climate are less than 3 degree Celsius. Due to intense surface heating and high humidity, cumulus and cumulonimbus clouds form early in the afternoons almost every day. The daily day temperature is about 32 degree Celsius, while the night time temperatures averages to 22 degree Celsius.

A climatologist is the name given to a person who has extensively studied climatology.

Dry Climate

The most obvious climatic feature of this climate is that potential evaporation and transpiration (giving off moisture) exceeds precipitation (rainfall). These climates extend from 20 – 35 degree north and south of the equator and in large continental regions of the mid-latitudes often surrounded by mountains. Minor types of this climate include:

Dry arid (desert) is a true desert climate. It covers 12 per cent of the Earth's land surface and is dominated by xerophytic vegetation.

Astonishing fact

Warm near the equator and cold at the poles, our planet is able to support a variety of living things because of its diverse regional climates. The average of all these regions makes up Earth's global climate.

Dry semi arid (steppe) is a grassland climate that covers 14 per cent of the Earth's land surface.

Humid Subtropical Mid-latitude Climates

This climate generally has warm and humid summers with mild winters. Its extent is from 30 to 50 degree latitude mainly on the eastern and western borders of most continents. During the winter, the main weather feature is the mid-latitude cyclone. Convective thunderstorms dominate the summer months.

Astonishing fact

The Tundra climate consists of only two seasons— winter and summer. The region is frozen for the most part of the year. The average temperatures range from -28 degrees Celsius to -50 degrees Celsius.

Regional climate is the average weather pattern in a place for over more than thirty years, including the variations in seasons.

Moist Continental Mid-latitude Climates

Moist continental mid-latitude climates have warm to cool summers and cold winters. The average temperature of the warmest month is more than 10 degree Celsius, while the coldest month is less than -3 degree Celsius. Winters are severe with snowstorms, strong winds, and bitter cold from Continental Polar or Arctic air masses.

Astonishing fact

On April 14, 1986 Bangladesh was hit by the biggest hail stones ever recorded weighing over 1kg each, killing 92 people.

Polar Climate

Polar climates have year-round cold temperatures with the warmest month less than 10 degree Celsius. Polar climates are found on the northern coastal areas of North America, Europe, Asia and on the landmasses of Greenland and Antarctica. Two minor climate types exist—**Polar tundra and polar ice caps**. Polar tundra is a climate where the soil is permanently frozen to depths of hundreds of metres, a condition known as **permafrost**. Vegetation is dominated by mosses, lichens, dwarf trees and scattered woody shrubs. **Polar ice caps** have a surface that is permanently covered with snow and ice.

While the weather can change in just a few hours, climate changes over longer timeframes. Climate events, like El Nino, happen in several years, small-scale fluctuations happen over decades, and larger climate changes happen over hundreds and thousands of years.

Test Your MEMORY

1. What is atmosphere?
2. Name the layers of the atmosphere?
3. Write two lines about the thermosphere.
4. What is the ozone layer?
5. What is the importance of the ionosphere?
6. What is weather?
7. Name the different types of weather.
8. What is coastal weather?
9. What are the instruments used to measure weather?
10. What is climate?
11. What is the Köppen climate classification system?
12. Name the different types of climate.

Index